PRAISES FOR DAVID OMER BEARDEN

"Somewhere between Blake, Hank Williams and Homer, David Omer Bearden traveled a poetic line and gave himself over to it. 'To waltz is to leave without paying', he says in one poem. 'Which undermine all noble arrangements', he says in another. Bearden is one of those poets who begins an old man and gets younger as he progresses. Out of time all of the time, the window he shares with us allows us both a view into his poems and a view of him. Born in Blythe, California, raised in the 40s and 50s, senses sharpened in the 60s and 70s. Who has time for a career when you're studying the line this hard? 'I set fire to bitter walking papers./I was ever the I am not in those good days.' *The Mental Traveler* brings the reader into the sharp, sardonic and gorgeous observations of this fine bard that we may '. . . interpolate him into here/flash-drowning world/one moment/before the blink.' Poetry has always had a home for the outsider, and David Bearden waits there now, his poems in your hands."

— *Edmund Berrigan*

D1219913

"It is clear that David Omer Bearden took himself very seriously. It is equally clear that he also took the craft of poetry and the world he created with his poetry seriously. . . There is an autobiographical component to this work as a whole, and often specifically. . . We are taken on a wide and deep journey through his life, exposed often to his negative responses to his environment. Yet, his descriptions of the desert flora around Blythe, California and various places in Oklahoma show by eloquent detail, his constant sensitivity to his environment. . . One cannot read these poems without realizing you are in the presence of an important poet. His ability to illuminate a landscape with notes of emotive description is superb. One soon realizes that this is ingrained in the body and mind of this poet and his unique renderings of his observations are far purer than stylized. His mind and his craft seem to be one."

— *Roxie Powell*

"David Omer Bearden's work speaks to the traveller in all of us and touches on a kind of allusion found in the poets I love: Rimbaud & Lorca; with the sensuality of Neruda. He creates these authentic images of places that feel like out of memory or in a Terrence Malick film; somewhere between the sacred and the mundane. . . Bearden is one of those important poets whose voice is unique and in the long tradition of the great written word going back to the Ancient Greeks."

— *Nicholas Tolkien*

"Poets sometimes explode with radiance and then die young. This is the romantic model that so appeals to the sophomoric, but which is not a literary necessity. In David Omer Bearden's case, he burned bright and early, intimidated his colleagues, and then continued to survive, getting painfully battered the way life does to everybody. The upside of living a long life as a poet may be that suffering ceases to be an aesthetic foundation for preciousness, and becomes the coin of the realm. In a great poet's life, the drubbings of experience cut far deeper than with ordinary mortals. It becomes a miracle of creation when the infrequent psychic alchemy occurs which transmutes ugly experience into beautiful Art."

— *Dion Wright*

"Bearden's earlier poems are full of neo-surreal descriptions, with elaborate images, and intimate know-how of American lingo. His most recent identity as a 'traveler' focuses more directly and with strong success on lyrical, romantic themes of love, friendship, and family. As a fellow poet, I admire his ability to access and phrase as achieved in the title poem. 'And the wayfaring traveller; For ever open is his door. . . Till he becomes a wayward Babe, And she a weeping Woman Old, Then many a Lover wanders here; The Sun and Stars are nearer roll'd'"

— *Gerd Stern*

THE MENTAL TRAVELER

POEMS OF DAVID OMER BEARDEN

EDITED BY ASTRA BECK

Rosace Publications

The Mental Traveler pays homage to William Blake's poem of the same title*,
& was compiled in part from these chapbooks by David Omer Bearden:

SO LONG AT THE FAIR & DOWN AT THE PALOMINO CLUB
& OTHER POEMS. *Larkspur, 1976.*

THE ROSACE IN A STAR CHAMBER. *Sonoma, 1981.*

REDRESS. (A Solace Codex). *Seattle, 1983.*

All these books were brought out by Rosace Publications.

Individual poems are undated — tickets punched Eternity outside on Time.

Some of these poems (many in earlier versions) appeared in these journals:
Burning Bush, "C", Changes, Cold Spring Journal, The Columbia Review,
The Columbia Spectator, Fux, The Irregular Quarterly, LeFeuDuCiel, Love Lights,
Mondo Hunkamooga, Nadada, Nimrod, Now, Now Now, Our Conscious Love,
Out Of Sight, San Fernando Poetry Review, Telephone,
Underground Telegram, The Villager, The White Dove Review

Roundup into manuscript completed January 20, 1990.
First edition published in the United States in 2018 by Rosace Publications.

Cover photograph at Tulúm by Dion Wright

Drawing "The Traveller hasteth in the Evening" by William Blake, 1793,
provided by Yale Center for British Art, Paul Mellon Collection

Photographs by James Bearden (pp. 30, 54, & 98)

Book design by Astra Beck

Cataloging-in-Publication Data is available from the Library of Congress

Printed in the United States of America
Library of Congress Control Number: 2017964737
ISBN 978-0-9997777-0-1 (paperback)

www.davidbearden.com

* *Appendix D*

Acknowledgments

Special thanks to Edgar Owen & Microsoft Word at *Mindsun*,
Johanna & Astra, Barbara Arnofsky & WordStar.

*Astra Beck would like to specially thank
Dion Wright, Robert Dumont, James Bearden,
Aaron Kemble, & Theresa Beck for their support, faith,
& advice in releasing this long-awaited book.*

for the great Johanna

TABLE OF CONTENTS

"It is not permitted to proffer the disaster account."
— William Seward Burroughs

The Traveller hasteth in the Evening.
— *William Blake*

FOREWORD

Life is unfair. Perhaps not entirely a cheat, but readers of this collection will agree, thus far David Bearden has been cheated out of his rightful place in poetry's canon. No blame for this can we cast on any particular doorstep. The fault lies nowhere, not even in America's current tragic disregard for the profound lyric. This loss seems more ethereal, roiling in the mists and craggy geographies of Greek mythology, cast about the salt-green seas of Odysseyan wandering. For David Bearden breathed, a rhapsodist, as one among the ancient Greeks, a wandering minstrel reciting a fully lived contemporary epic.

He intoned an existence so utterly dedicated to verse that his attention to bodily needs and comforts allowed barely enough for daily survival. Sojourning from place to place, the scarcity of his possessions mirrored those of a Zen monk, but one immersed in the quixotic grit of American culture. His treasure was the language, the marvelous lexicon he carried in his head. His contemporaries were the Beats, of the Beatitudes, poets and writers, and in that tradition of singular voices Bearden's speaks a passion to detail that explores with x-ray then microscopic vision the rarely investigated interiors of ordinariness. While equally his words float like planetary fragments, eclectic references weaving particular towns, artists, brand names, celestial bodies, fictional icons, and a literary recall, as brilliant as any ever written, into our quotidian. In each instance his evidence blasts open the commonplace to reveal a cosmic infinitude, dark to us before. But Bearden's true genius quivers in a play of abstractly connected images sewn together with such tenderness, that reading, we feel the needle in our very cloth.

His topics are taboo and honky tonk. Searing with human frailty lines bleed into raw metaphor and crazy times unfolding. He comes up through small town emptiness, vagabond opiated, rich in lingo transforming. He could finger a lyre like a razor peeling away vapidness. But most of all there is a hunger. An insatiable poetic visionary hunger fused to a power of descriptive intensity that sends us whirling in a sea of burning stars.

— Maureen Owen

EDITOR'S PREFACE

My mother introduced me to David in the fall of 1985 when I was five years old. I remember clearly his tousled salt and pepper hair, and that he was wearing a long khaki raincoat. He greeted me with a warm handshake and smile, and said: "Hello, I'm David, nice to meet you." From there on out David was my friend and teacher, letting me run wild with imagination and a free spirit. He encouraged poetry, music, art, and how to see beauty in the brandless and humor in the brand. Our love for one another was unconditional and deepened as he was a part of our family for over 20 years right up until he passed.

Looking back now, I realize the rarity and genius behind David's matrix and how he is an important legacy to our American literature that should not be forgotten. To my surprise, one day I came across a stack of papers tucked away inside the flap of David's briefcase. It was his unpublished manuscript: The Mental Traveler — dedicated to my mother Johanna. I remember David talking about this manuscript for years and how he had misplaced it somewhere. I am excited to have uncovered these lost papers, because I knew this should be the first book of his to publish while celebrating his work and life.

Publishing The Mental Traveler was a labor of love and a project that became inconceivably supported by many people. I am grateful and honored to have connected with so many of David's colleagues and associates who have helped make this book come to be. The Mental Traveler has widened my perspective beyond the mundane and is a treasure left behind for literary discovery.

— Astra Beck

Twin boys, David & Daniel Bearden, Blythe, California

PROEM
A BABY FABLE

"Fuck around & rest up", the kid reckoned, fallen close to sleep beside the quiet silver body of Rosenda. Foggy eve crept into Vacaville. O yeah, the kid mused how outside his window high school kids cruised the hot streets, some in long finned icebox white Caddys, safety pinned in tresses & sea blue body shirts. He hoped his stepdaughter was not necessarily tripping with these; hoped rather she was part of the pride of some young lion, nourished perhaps on Moloko plus. Then he recalled with a start of horror the curse he labored under, & lay back recollecting . . .

Story from somewhere else invisible & congruent of Uncle Luke starting to his feet when Uncle Chet announced the birth of twins, only to impale himself on the spike of an ornate iron lamp directly through the closed fontanelle of his small, balding head. The crimson spurt, a baffled cry, & Lucre fell to the tile floor passing away, who once had wakened from a bender to see himself in a peeling silver mirror the powerful Lord of Animal Complacency . . .

Would it give some soldier out there a rush to know the kid had a recurring dream of outrunning an hydrophobic mandrill across vacant lots of shattered plumbing like busted ceramic hearts slippery in a downpour? At last, blood & rain water mingled in his eyes, came walking back to a clearing in familiar shaggy trees. The crepuscule . . . violet sky sprent with clear white desert stars high over pale cottonwoods . . . & through gray needles of a tall salt cedar, the red hot pinprick of Mars . . . in a kind of porch swing secured among great cottonwood boughs sat Uncle Chet, in livery of leisure identical to that of Uncle Lucre, who reclined on the ground in a talc of alkali, in khaki fedora, shirt & trousers. Luke however, sported a pencil-line mustache. Chet passed a flat pint bottle of Four Roses bourbon whiskey to his crony, who took an enormous slash, gasped & spoke:

"You know yourself, Chet, these new ones coming up is not like you are me. You seen they cain't carpenter. By God I believe we're the last real carpenters left."

*"You prob'ly right," Uncle Chet agreed, & lay back in the swing. Lucre rose
& reeled over to an off-white Ford pickup truck, much worked & battered,
cursing apathy & fatigue in a drawled mumble, climbed over into the chill
iron bed & passed out.*

*"You should never have lived in images," the appalling visage of Chango
grinned, even as he conjured the ghost of Humphrey Bogart to help him light
his Lucky Strike.*

The kid nodded in his sleep, "O yeah, yeah I see now how that's lethal . . ."

*Now o'erthrown kid Prospero picks up any telephone to hear his last pal's
lady on the party line. But don't you shill for the assassin kid; unbearable
moments emit that. Stay up on this razor's edge; — the ark of human soul on
a lake of fire. A kid's revery you see . . . he was gazing into the old House of
Abraham now, & seeing the Barabbas fable too . . . to know & carry all is
what this kid could have . . .*

*"Fuck and Die", read melancholy Nellie on the water closet wall. As she
sat thus, her painful labor began, til she cried out. Chet leapt from the
swing like a vigilante, drunk as a Lord but instantly alert through his blood,
sobered by Nellie's cry. He ran across to the concrete bath house, where in the
verdigrised shower stalls his voice rang out & echoed "Sis! Where in Hell
you at?" Finding her moaning & near, he swept Nellie's heavy Venusian body
up in his arms, carried her at a swift stiff-backed walk over the hard dirt of
the Okie compound, past the Pullman Caboose up on blocks to the pickup,
& maneuvered expertly fast through oiled dust streets, gripping a clear
knob containing a red rose bud, to the little Mexican Mission hospital. Luke
was coming to in back.*

*A brace of boys were born to Nellie, hard delivered, She cried, swooning,
waking & dreaming. She heard in her popped ears the loud earthunder.
Little buds come waxy on the hide of Mother. Caves above the river gape.
The clotted milky way flows. Coyotes out on the mesas yipped & barked at
a bone moon. Withered tamaracks & cottonwoods muttered like elder men.
Around midnight red & white babies frowning in the hollow of her great arms,
she lay back exhausted, smoke already in her Irish hair damp brown on the
pillow, faint edema in her face, & sighed, "Chester, I brung twin sons into
this old world."*

*The world in the West of it, where a man could get used to dense night in slot
bardo, if the crowd come, or he could get some sleep. & Uncle Chet too fond*

to tell her Lucre bloodied in the waiting room . . . & Wintertime, a cold wave high as the sky swept out of the desert into hick town of Blythe & froze corpses of cats & dogs under houses. No one had broken through.

Wind blew sand & alkali through creaking salt cedar limbs & cotton-woods where a porch swing yawed in its chains; stung pitted walls of the communal bath house, the wretched boxcars huddled on blocks; sheetrock & tarpaper of Omer & Nellie's bedroom, newly annexed to the caboose which served as the long Bearden living room, where a window extended cakes of yellow light. Here Omer slumped that early morning in halos of Saturn, before a Westinghouse console radio set, still in his soiled white carpenter's overalls. Stations drifted into one another . . . Mexican falsetto from far away south faded to loud Guy Lombardo dance music . . . The Shadow's sounding laughter broke through a newscaster's deadpan rap . . . some cowboy intoned behind quavering steel guitars how he was so sorry if he broke somebody's heart . . . static . . . lighting out on the pan of the Mojave . . . Omer sat in his chair, pitifully humbly frowning at nothing, too tired to rise & tune the radio . . .

THE FROWNING BABE

In what testament could he confess
how at birth he was transported
to slaughterhouse rafters
never to go home never
but that a pure calf
was butchered near his tiny soul
& the falling rain of blood
robbed his twin of substance

leaving immaculate pinned diapers
empty booties tied with real ribbon
a little crib in a shabby living room
two anxious, jovial troglodytes
& a naked human baby on beams
hung with the drenched,
degraded beasts?

WHOM?

whose microMegas?

What spirit is little David before a protest is needed?
> when he bit into the shortbread only to
> desperate sobs of *"it's bwoke, it's bwoke"*,
> & his despair impossible for old Nellie to assuage,
& he got fever, —
> so that his tiny fists clenched his under shift
> in must of an earthly cot, his new eyes glitter —
> bubble reflecting Eternity containing Infinity
> pulsing in unspeakable sensation of birth of
> Smallest-Greatest shivering concept . . .
When he raved colicky of a Giant
> who lived among the great sunflowers by the road;
> blooms exploding the burning noon; the Giant's
> compound face of live sun-drinking bumps
> senses the bright atoms boiling in a violent blonde radiance,
> that sharp smell of sunflowers forever . . .
"O I hear dogs barking Mama far away barking from
> *farm to farm in the dark out there are they*
> *barking at the Giant what do they want Mama?"*
Now the dogs hush, the Palo Verde Valley lies silent
> the river's current dimples, flowing deep . . .
What spirit is finding breath of inhabited sleep, frail
> with a freshening fever,
> while over the distant highway grade
> the down-shifting, lugging, grinding
> Diesels go?
What consciousness saw the men in khaki chase the dog
> under the railroad boxcars on blocks & shoot it
> again & again passing a .22 rifle as it snarled &
> yelped & banged against pipes & boards
> & then became still. (Deadpan adults showed home a
> crushed egg with an unborn
> chick packed wetly in, torn by the dog's teeth,
> broken shell smeared with strange sepia blood . . .)

Who strutted before the women who stood by in hick
　　　　print dresses worried that the killing of the dog
　　　　would traumatize the baby boy, — but he is playing
　　　　like he's a man, firing a toy
　　　　machine gun that you crank . . .
What sustained the horror the women looked for
　　　　in the deep eyes, but could not detect because
　　　　it was hidden under a compulsive swagger
　　　　that knew it lied to the women . . . ?
What quiet face was that with a blurred rose
　　　　blot, or birthmark, smiling a Jupiter in the
　　　　outer dark pressing on the window
　　　　if old Omer couldn't see it, or dismissed it as
　　　　a wanderer, some hobo from the jungle by the tracks,
& he pulled off his soiled white overalls
　　　　with weary unconscious gestures,
　　　　famished for his night of calm sleep . . . ?
Whose soul at that moment felt itself
　　　　alone from everyone
　　　　in the whole world, if the Daddy sat on the edge
　　　　of a disheveled bed, denying the enormous
　　　　countenance,
　　　　& barely glancing at the window . . . ?

HOUR OF NONES

for Stephen W. Hawking

Morning hummed waxy
in his ears. He couldn't
make a fist. Baby phlegm
stood in his throat. He did
Dad's hawk & lunger.
He jumped from bed,
his lids sticking.
He was mad to rush outside,
to trip & fall.
This little boy got ready
for school, saturating
his cowlick with Fitch rose hairoil.
A lace breaks on wingtip
shoes with oddly worn heels.
Because his homework was undone
he swooned into a savage dream
in Pal-ul-don by Edgar Rice Burroughs
on the space-swept savannahs
of the walk to school.
Brute-visaged men with the bodies
of ponies carried faint girls
with rosy nipples & blue-black hair
afar off, vanishing
on the real horizon
of palms & canals of Blythe,
appearing sinewy & barbarous
& loud in the kid's daymare, —
far overhead a hawk...
along a sidewalk a spilled lunch blew, —
bruised pink banana,
white mayonnaises in the sky,
light bread & thin red soup...
His slumber full
circled. He was thrilled as a kid.
He turned home inside
to sit in Daddy's chair. Hearing sobbing
jibbering bugs of the woodwork.

The real horizon & the daytime moon
sober a child. His round little face
touching the breeze
in space feels the slow
entire of the present, —
walking body beneath blue sky
a desert valley morning,
heat of homework hardly begun.
Primordial savannahs of lots
of Johnson grass & rank arrow-weeds
to dunes ending
in the lane of cottonwood trees...
Blythe, California. Shining white sand,
phosphenes, teeming hills of big red ants,
a crawling yellow cowkiller,
oiled dirt streets. A clear blister
forming on his heel.
A grownup somnambulist trudges by.
Grammar school bell
in a de Chirico mission.
A kid with wild but lazy
overcharges in his nerves
hurried out. Space was everywhere
full of clear vitreous floaters.
& as day blissed through
to heaven through salt cedars,
he heard the droll iron bell tolling
the hour of nones.

VOICE

I know the best trick you ever saw,
but it must be done at the end of one's rope,
at the last ditch touching the last straw
to the spark fading within the cinder hope . . .

When peace like a river wonder gives up
the wonderful words of fish, shepherds labor
their sheep where cross the crowded ways of life,
& the voice I hear falling in my ear
none other has ever known.

Prayer for articulation
prayer of secret exultation song
there is a glory in our souls brother
the little flowers peep through to a land
beyond the reason river as you know.

2 September 1964

PSALM

In Tulsa, where the stench of oil will swell
Under the flickering basement-ceiling clouds
& make one sick, my soul throve fitfully.
Where Oral Roberts' tower of ormolu
Proves to the poor a wonder-working power,
& bitch success litters her engineer —
Smart sons in school & presbytery,
I soothed my soul with the red medicine-mud
As in a sheepcote of my own young age,
& ate peyote on some crinoid rocks
Above the indian-given town
Like Nazarite or decadent Osage,
Singing *"O mind's rosace! O wormwood star!*
Caseharden my ironic proud-flesh heart
That I may find the manly excellence!
You bitter light! My weird six-pointed shield
Shines in a sick abyss of mania
Like a confusing fever, if I lack
Light-gathering, resolving strength!"
Walking among sea-lilies turned to stone,
I sang to Tulsa's stored-up horns of oil
Acred below me on the Arkansas:
"I go with arms outstretched, to touch the hide
Of (stalking at my side), my Lion-Self!"
Refinery volcanoes banked their fires,
Smoking the louring basement-ceiling sky;
But ancient starlight seeped into my eyes
As the red mud upon my forehead broke,
& I was hushed, to hear my bleating sheep. *Selah.*

ON THE PALE CRIMINAL

It is smooth
& bone white as that gull
against the darkening thunderheads,
or creamy as Nefertiti's inner thighs,
or agony peach,
or off white as the belly of a toad
turned over on his back
by a boy playing God . . .

Cold phosphorous pebbles
of gypsum stone
gleam in the dark humus
beneath the old blood
of the night roses . . .

It shines
as the fresh complexion
of the moon . . .

It is crystalline
as those glittering ceilings
the Okies blow onto sheetrock…
Pearly as tapioca beads,
empty as an eggshell
amphora in the shadowed corner
of a tomb
where the princess Ananka waits
sleeping,
wound in the mummy cloth . . .

It is a field of dark blue snow
or roseate as frosted milk
glass holding wine.
It is heavy light.

MARKS OF THE BEAST

1.

"Bind us in time, O Seasons clear, and awe.
O Minstrel galleons of Carib fire,
Bequeath us to no earthly shore until
Is answered in the vortex of our grave
The seal's wide spindrift gaze toward paradise."
      — Hart Crane

That one is a comic
existential bog of bones
with witch's hammer, —
stinking pissing shet
down in Sappho's mustaches
where mule foals
a light wait away . . .
& sadder than the walrus' eyes
you red heels of the old regime,
Chango in Yemaya
watching sidewalking hermit the pink
segmented exoskeletons of mute baby,
little peri the manatee safety pin & vary
with celluloid parrot as Holy Ghost,
penny sows, sea-hares, crawling satanic mutillids,
& King Cecrops bumping his eyes
off against the light.
See society, —
see the centaur
ants teaming in the remains of a fox . . .
all seized from the sky, gentle witness, —
as ammonia wafts from the crabs
& the ruins are walking away . . .
Apocalypse monsoon
came from foreign places,
& the tormented sea chops on
under its sway
on her free journey
in the face of the dim
luminous moon
become as blood.

2.

"... from faces fallen on inertia ground
the rot we must avoid."
                    — Blair H. Allen

& this animal has a hawk's gaze
louring on the heavy weakened shoulder
of a lucky reprobate bull
whom the crowd pics: "Give us Barabbas!"
Jesus watched
from the black holes
in his exhaustion.
See the flashing beak peck down, —
Jack Abbott stepping into Dick Adan.
Hard eyes stone a tattooed woman
into a wintry grave beneath cold stars.
Or some sweet esoteric letter comes
with just the right shade of show you
ashes of your one true love
scattered at last on the sea.
Dead pan Charlie takes care of Nedra Eb.
Beatrice blew some guy a lying kiss.
Machiavelli high-grades all the young arrivals
entering his cold blue ken to please.
Apocalypse talons fall
& rise above new roses
spattering this shore,
gentle witness. — See
how pride would not let murder go
leaving life's honor perhaps alone
praying to the infinite
high indifference?

San Fernando Valley
January 1983

THE BLACK HOTEL

Visiting the Okie poet's room
to smoke hashish & listen through the walls,
I heard each human sound heroically —
comprehending the hallway messages:
Next door four fingers cantered like a horse,
a chair scraped out the pensioner's short cough,
& gentle wheezing was a distant broom . . .
Then I heard anger mounting the high stair
in stiff footfalls! I opened the door a crack
to see a deep-black negro stride the hall's
length swiftly, pausing before a door
at key & lock. His step was urgent sound
expressing low what you will understand
that I had overheard with walking ears!

He flicked his glance to me like grabbing flies,
& I saw tarter darken his eye-whites.
In my sensitive trance I heard his voice erupt
as the dull hall light, particle & wave,
polished dark tortoise plates of his locked skull,
& poured like cocoa down his molten neck.
The sequence was the twinkling of an eye
wherein the black man made his statement there,
glancing, turning a knob, . . . & left the hall
of fevered light on a conscious knowledge.
The tiny barnacles along his jaw!
His sound was wrathful thunder rising!
The words themselves broke from him utterly —
"Every Damned Dog Will Have His Day."

Lower East Side
New York City

Baby brother James & David Bearden, Blythe, California

FOR MY BABY BROTHER

"Nay, Son of Man, I have been lifted up.
To Thee I rose like a rocket ending in mid-heaven.
But even thou, Son of Man, canst not quaff out the dregs of
  terrestrial manhood!
They fall back from Thee."
  — D.H. Lawrence

1.

I too have a cheeseburger jones, —
Remember McDaniel's where the roof was corrugated tin,
& when the family went in, we exchanged looks
Like between James Beard & Julia Child
At the exquisite bouquet of chili & batter for prawns
As the rotating fan riffled the unnow lace
of the white curtains
On the drywalls?
Big, round, generous enriched buns
Of light bread, wonder bread, studded, were they,
With brown, parched sesame seeds?
Open, in any case, & larded high
With more than a quarter lb. of seared black beef
Gooey with molten gold of American cheese; —
& let me tell you son, when the lacey fringe
Is hard & crispy from the iron grill,
& this sharp frill is soaked in chili juice
From the big ladle of beans, it's something else!
The lid is smeared with sweet bulk mayonnaise,
To which the iceberg lettuce sticks,
& the cold crimson juices of tomatoes sliced
Leak & entwine with sour vinegar wine
Of big dill chips of pickle that blow your mind . . . !
Remember, Jim? This was a chiliburger,
Cheeseburger of eternity, after total immersion
Church on bleakest Baptist Sundays,
The one good earthly jewel that we knew!
So wash it down with gulps of chocolate shake,
But douse that sucker with catsup Jim,
For every baby goes, & that was years ago . . .

2.

How fuckin trashy can it get?
Blythe, California sheetrock room,
Too much desert sun through opening windows
In big open Window for any real comfort,
Afternoon glare of horrible pop music
On the Westinghouse console: —
"Mockingbird Hill" by Patti Page,
tra la la tweedle de de dee
it gives me a thrill . . .
Horrible! Worse than *"Second Hand Rose"*,
Heard years later
In a jungle wet with rain . . .
The awful emptiness
Of those pointblank desert afternoons!
Walking to town
Feeling strange, light as those golden shells
Of cicadas stuck all over the cottonwoods, —
Feeling a terror a kid shouldn't know
Anything about . . .
At the Palo Verde Drug I'd buy a sleazy fix:
American cheese sandwich on white
With mayonnaise & lettuce & a Coca Cola . . .
Back in my body again far as such fare
Could nourish me . . .

Jesus Saviour pilot me!

A CENTERPIECE

for Charles Plymell
(Psalms 2:12)

Smooth fruit posed in a bowl
arranged for looks, with awned wheat heads
stickering out. Eyes were alright,
they saw the apple of the eye,
pear-bell & grape,
but mind did not do well
imagining how sealed, how carefully
the melon's center heart, the apple's core
is closed about by fiber which organically
inserts no door

A seedy spirit known as through a rind
ingrows in the firm quick of this stillife;
stuff grown harmoniously & lawfully
& not unkind
but awful to this mind, welded & dumb.
What empathy (touching the even sheen)
for melons & the like feels the aesthete,
seeing his agony in mouthless fruit or grain; —
in the taut place around black apple seeds
& tight in tiny khaki pearls of wheat.

THE DESK IS A FROZEN SEA
& HE STRAINS TO SING ABOUT TIME & AGE
ALAS HIS HEART WILL BREAK IN THREE
& A LINE TRICKLES OUT ONTO THE PAGE:

He dozes & dreams for miles
of white sea-ice, which he must limp across
needing badly to ease his bowels
knotted like frozen clods. So soon he squats

in an embarrassing wind
baring himself, & saying, "Let me shet.
O God, why do you make me whine
in pain for any birth?" The place he sits

is terrible ice, & coldly
cut by the thin wind which does not sing.
So straining and hurt at that pole
he makes one tortured turd which tears & hangs

bleeding into the blank snow.
It lives! It is strung with throbbing black veins!
He touches it & whimpers: "O
God, this horror twined with my own membrane

is shame! Pain with no defense!
I take from my pack my critical knife
& sever this experience,
of which I'll never speak, if I survive!"

SHAME*

by Arthur Rimbaud
translated by Judith & David Bearden
Hired hand's house, Ramelli Ranch, Plumas County

So long as the razor has
Not amputated that brain,
That packet of white & green fat,
Whose vapors are never fresh,

(Ah! He ought to cut loose from his
Nose, his lips, his ears,
His paunch! & fairly abandon
His laigs! O marvel!)

But no; really, I guess as long
As the blade to his head,
The stones to his side,
& the fire to his guts,

Haven't executed him, the baby
So wearisome, the so stupid beast,
Mustn't cease for an instant
To pull ruse & betray,

& like some Rockies' wildcat
Stink up all spheres!
But still, when he dies, O my God!
May some prayer rise up!

* Appendix A

SHINING MIRROR

Again he comes
unto the beryl & silver
glass; — opening window on the other world
he watches silently, It makes him shiver,
as the little child confronts the wold, —
as a ghost beard drifts from the moon
across the sleeping face of himself,
& fear comes.
   . . . Wolf eye that frightened Stephen holds home now.

ZARZUELA

Cantina "La Cuna"

See faded blue cover of billiard table with new silver peso glued onto it . . . stand felt up & slide it back quickly until it is sky world . . . you with a bright migraine touched by flutter of air . . . glance to open window of distance in adobe wall to see coin moon . . . summer dusk . . . puddles in streets fill with luminous orange water . . . horizon is light gray hill showing word *XIPE* in strings of white stone . . . turn back to room . . . a sullen Mexican musician serenades a whore & her American john . . . the musician fixes the john in a gaze of pure *Macho* hate, but sings these words to their mournful melody:

"Con dinero o sin dinero,
hago siempre lo que quiero
Y mi palabra es la ley;
No tengo trono ni reina,
ni nadien que me comprenda
Pero sigo siendo el Rey."

then he takes a greenback from the man, says something to the impassive indian whore, & takes his leave . . . see indian whore . . . fat American speaks to her . . . she sits in yellow glare from niche above her . . . from sky blue part down center of her scalp black hair falls to smooth shoulders in close tiny waves glistening with pomade . . . pale yellow halo stands about her head . . . eyebrows scrolls of black grease . . . she reflecting festering cheese man in obsidian eyes cut cabochon . . . her vast lips smile labia pink . . . rose . . . glimpse of purple tissue . . . mouth dry from marijuana . . . sips water . . . smoke slowly coiling up . . . her eyes close, the lids lipsticked thickly red . . . watch fat man pass finger on brow . . . flick sweat on heavy damp wall . . . woman opens eyes . . . man speaks, grinning . . . woman pulls man's limp shirt from crease where belly-rolls lip public bulge . . . he seizes her hand, places her fingers against chino trousers at crotch . . . staring the while . . . where nipples of enormous teats are clasped by dingy white dress . . . cleavage flesh moist with Solomon oil . . . she looks down upon his damp round tonsure . . . sandy hair, thin . . . See *glans penis* against upper thigh . . . she has finger at his leg . . . moving blood-shellac fingertip on bulge . . . cock straining . . . wet squoze asshole . . . your mouth of gnashing gears in yam gruel . . . wired eyes . . . his heel taps tiled floor . . . spinning coin coming to a stop . . . they burst into laughter . . . she making scornful *"ahhhhh"* . . . with rising inflection . . . he strangles *"gohod god eee"* . . . his short hands grip knees . . . she smiling strokes his cock, raising thin whorled eyebrows . . . he

bends forward from waist . . . sighing . . . see suddenly her impassive face
. . . cheekbones raised high by yellow light . . . take a drink of water . . . stunned
furniture . . . head splitting . . . she raises white dregs to her lips . . . they stand,
woman smoothing rayon dress over belly, navel a slack disk in cambered flesh
. . . fat man holds shirtail between thumb & forefinger . . . come has glued
cotton shorts . . . your eyes delicious egg whites . . . mouth filling with clear
gruel . . . you are asleep . . . long bar deserted . . . unfired bowls of red clay
hold dry lemons . . . she is walking through a wide door . . . black courtyard of
puddles . . . fat American follows her thin calves of fine black hair . . . sunken
in mirror your wan face . . . jungle murals of muscular blue orchids, pastel
moccasin flowers . . . palmettos lift their hands, bamboo & dense fig leaves
. . . small in the background a wild Stag flees away through thickets . . . buggy
rose trees, gangs of marmoset & howler monkeys . . . lianas climb, flowery
vines depend from titanic mahogannies . . . blur of a hummingbird, bright
canaries & paroquets . . . emerging head of purple & gray water snake makes
silver rings on a black pool . . . a gorgeous silkworm moth, its wide wings
each with a crescent moon edged in red, flexes on blowzy orange poincianas
. . . amber owl eyes glow among dark verdure . . . niches in wall hold gleaming
ceramic images of Virgin Mary lighted with garish blonde blubs . . . streaks
of hard red fingernail enamel down serene countenance . . . sky of black felt
. . . migraine fever . . . transparent chains of dead cells drifting down . . . sullen
musician returns to the strange room, leans mosaic mother-of-pearl inlaid
guitar against bar . . . light short shirt sleeves . . . looking out a far window
. . . woman & fat America float from courtyard . . . smell of laundry drains . . .
cilantro . . . she has smoked . . . her face serene, streaked with sweat . . . sullen
Mexican touches guitar . . . sings in soft falsetto . . .

"No vale nada la vida, la vida no vale nada.

Comienza siempre llorando Y
asi llorando se acaba;
por eso es que en este mundo,
la vida no vale nada..."

Fat man looks away from his whore . . . you in that mind ripples of shiny
black hair spread on flat brown pillow . . . you are asleep fitfully wide mouth
. . . breasts stained nipples . . . spittle . . . sobbing American sees glittering far
Aztec eyes looking at larval fat fucking her sucking her . . . nostrils clog with
heavy apple musk . . . fat man walks to a wide door . . . enters night . . . moon
of a sugar skull floating . . . slowly dissolves in wet wind of sky wide mouth . . .

Songs: "El Rey" & "Camino De Guanajuato" by Jose Alfredo Jimene

OUTSKIRTS

"What we've been doing . . .
     Mother, it must stop! Now,
          I'm not asking;
You are being told! The shapes we make!
     in the deep middles
          of these beds . . . I'm through!
Those weird motels   THE GROVE   THE MOONLITE
          & your great breasts hanging
          like obfuscous moons . . .

Stop staring like an owl
     Mother! I'm cutting out.
          . . . Very tired of out old trips
     from Ulro to L.A.,
          caressing as we do in nightly rooms!
I'll have the goddamn coffee brought,
          then I'll go out
hitch-hiking in a country where
          the burning sun pisses the wind!

You've kept me pale,
          sleeping on top always . . ."

HISTORY OF FISHES

There on the vague banks we heard
the river rush in our crushing
pubic bones. Kissing like fishes,
moaning deeper than our crossed throats . . .
Turning . . . turning so I got
rayon seat-cover burns on my knees . . .
Burning! Burning along the short black trickle
of our lives, Nedra . . . a ball of phosphor
left the poles along our legs,
the river's tendons sagged . . . I fell beside
that flow into a gracile field . . .
the grasses of your fine pudendal hair,
Nedra. Nedra . . .
The shock of the catching of our glances.
Our ears hearing the clogged radio sobbing
some sad boy's lyric, lost in the night pleroma . . .
We saw the night now, it was carbon paper.
A round bright glow above the banks
was God's cigar just burning through
Nedra Eb, sweet young child . . .
the glow had dulled to chalk even as we
walked beside the river...
vague banks . . . vague, dark river . . .
The trees were filled with shining fishes
young lovely child . . . Nedra
" . . . when they're quick in the deep,
why, all fish are asleep;
they swim in a trance, & spawn in a dream.
When they're caught, they awake
being horribly choked,
& drown with a soundless scream."

FIRE

Fire went away like *Xipe Totec*
She seemed a sketch. A Lautrec, half colored in
vermillions of freckles. Her hair was stiff as gas
    flares across the river
        & the same color as those flames.
Her eyebrows jumped the gap
when she sat in the cold wind of the ocean she made a conjuration.
    Scandinavian villages were glimpsed.
        Under her cape she was holding
        Viking medicine
& more stiff red hair & ice cream bars.
        I know her pockets were full. & her
hands were transparent, armed with brass
        claws like tiny mitres.
She danced into the fore front. She had power.
        Fire had the right. She was Tamar
        dancing. Her laughter was
Pregnant   Unhappy   Joyous   Valiant   Honest
        Desperate   Crazy
        I think men loved her. Girls
certainly loved her. Fire was torn up
with her weird victories…
        looking over her retinue of males
she longed for the big Greek, the Swede,
the one-eyed Tangerine, the methedrine hero.
        When she called Lauren on the phone
she glimpsed the nearly full moon out the loft
window & she began to scream. A hideous scream,
        like a loba, a bruja, Cassandra
        schizophrenic with her dark glass
          broken, drenched in benzine
            rinsings from the Moon. *(Crane)*
          & she said that The God
        was hooked on blood,
mad to see it burst from out its larval
containment, spurting down
        steps of the pyramid,
          the tenement stairs,
            the picked wound,

                    the Oedipal face . . .
I felt like falling in love with her. But who fell
            in that love? A negro boy named Light
            by her. Because he could titter
                when she screamed her pathic screams
on wrong speedballs of heroin & amphetamine,
            he was desperate,
                he was a Seminole indian too . . .
                Fire sitting naked
in the Moulin Rouge,
her skin of untouched canvas, white & grained.
            She is on a ship
                that trails a shattered moon.
Fire in Tanja, speaking Sufi with the muttering
Medjoub. She thrills me, I want to see her
            again in her cape of candy wrappers
            glued with chocolate. Fire!
                You fine foxy bitch!
            What are you doing? Is the Yellow sickness
            waiting for your descent?
What ruined house do you live in now?
            What do the Runes say?

KADILLAC KANDEE

Here is a true story for you.
I got to loving Kadillac Kandee
in an idiot honky tonk of Oklahoma
name of The Foos Roost.
Your mortal kids back in Wichita Kansas
& Tulsa Oklahoma
play this game
of foos ball a lot.
I mean it's a fad,
or was; —
some latinlike game
where one bats a little ball
past one's opponent
at a table.
Like in England it's pinball,
as it is for bus terminal punks
of America,
or was, before TV Pong.
In any case,
I'm wandering.
Actually, we first met
in Vicki's hot Wichita apartment
scoring for dilaudid.
Kandee looked like David Bowie,
with white skin I like,
fine bones,
& feathers like a bird.
I liked her at once.
She was a topless dancer
at a joint name of The Lemon Tree.
K.K. loved to nod
while she danced,
made love,
or shot dope, —
which things we did together
for a time.
Then we drove on down
to Tulsa for Christmas
in her estranged husband's

raked Chevy,
where I introduced her
to Alan Russo,
a burnt hearted poet
looking for a place
to function
you might say . . .
& Kadillac took us
down to the Foos Roost
but Alan wouldn't go in; —
he sat it out in the cold
car with a ski cap
pulled down over his ears
eating valiums & drinking
strawberry vodka,
because for one thing
he has not a mute cell
in his Rodin body.

Anyway,
so I fell in love with Kadillac Kandee
as she stood at the bar
under a black light,
hustling some guy she once knew
for smoke or something.
I recall some cowboy falling
to the floor
& someone saying
*"Get that man another
Tequila Sunrise!"*
Foos fools clicking,
things glowing white,
blue, moon, reds...
At that moment, watching her go
was when it happened, —
It was her sweet soaking tough
mama I loved
suddenly in the roost
we looked in one another's
eyes of apocalypse jade
sort of,

& laughed
at the highway.
Once we did crank,
went insane
& made love
for (c.) 4 hours.
Kandee was proud,
called it her world's record
for loving.
This was in Dennis' & my basement
on Erie Street in Wichita.
Dennis went to the county psycho ward...
O but first,
Dennis loved Kandee's friend, —
this hot little speed freak
with high smiles,
arches & tits
who also danced naked.
She showed me a poem
she wrote about first heartbreak
called *"Don't Ever Fall In Love M'Friend"*,
which I meant to publish
but lost among papers.
She was with Dennis on the night
the laws busted him driving insane
& threw him in the slammer; —
psycho ward.
They noted the stitches
on his wrists.
The young lady split
to Oklahoma City
where she came from.

So anyway,
me & Kandee lay
in bed all day, —
Kandee with long black
wig off
revealing coarse red hair
short shingled,
while she told me about the loss

of her baby girl,
the grief, — & how her husband wasn't
heavy enough for her,
& about how she'd fallen
from the days when she did
a little Red Riding Hood act
to the recorded accompaniment
of Sam the Sham & The Pharaoh's
"Hello Little Miss Riding Hood",
in a thin red cape
& pasties,
in some *"nice rooms"*,
as she put it.
You should have heard the way
she could pronounce the word
"Boots"; —
she had a pair of those
blue cowboy boots.

Kandee got popped
for something down in Tulsa,
& wound up committed
to an institution
exactly similar
to the one Dennis was in.
Haven't seen her since, —
had to run.
She was strong & beautiful
in a way;
one of the new foxes,
the diamond dogs & vixen, —
Something way gone with her
punched my heart . . .
I mean you could see,
looking up in her face,
how she'd been down
too soon, so hard . . .
I loved her, —
her sense of humor,
her acting too dramatic,
her perfect tits & legs.

I was 34,
she was 23 I think.
One time she wrote me a note
while I slept:
"You're a legend
in your own time.
You're a winner.
But nobody wins
in the end. Love,
Kandee."

Judee Sill & David Bearden, Mill Valley, California, 1973

THE VISIT

(with the late Judee Sill)

When I wrap you up in my arms & legs,
rocks melt & do the hula tenderly on little ginger feet;
the landlady upstairs has her first ecstasy,
to feel their tiny mary janes tapping on her cheeks.
when I kiss you,
poppies from planets of another dimension
burst everywhere in air,
& the world's ceiling cracks open wide,
to show them to us there.
When I hold your flaming ass,
a sun of butter clarifies in the heat of its breath,
& kamakazi bees dive into hearth milk for a sip
in sweet surrender, between the sheets.
When I plunge into your hair,
real perfumes entwine in perpetual counterpoint
for the instant the strange planets are close-up,
& citizens there whistle island songs in unison,
& eat small candy meteorites to show us
how to have fun.

Chelsea Cloisters, London

TOURING

England, Scotland & Oregon
(a joint diary with the late Judee Sill, 1973)

David: *Today (January 20) Judee & I leave to tour England. I'm 33 years old today. Flying 12 hours over arctic twilit cracked white sea in purple shadow. Forgive the northern sky its colored ices? Arrived in London. Simultaneously loving & using inner E-meter on Judee. This seat of Mars Archie Bunker calls a fag country. The streets seem to be full of beautiful tough young skinny people dressed fit to kill in the finery of the men of old. We walked around Soho . . .*

Judee: *David did great on both shows so far. He was more than generous to me on an interview. Tonight he made my cells explode with love . . .*

David: *Someday later (January 29) we saw William Burroughs walking on the old Bond Street. His face the light broke through . . . in "banker drag" . . .*

Judee: *Bought clothes, ate at Hiroko, and loved David a google or more to-day. Last night I had bad nightmares and threw up. David helped me. Today we are going to Portobello Road. I love David more and more desperately. I hope I don't go insane. Please. Tonight we did a show in Newcastle-Up-on-Tyne. David did great again. Tomorrow we go to Edinburgh Scotland. I love David more and more. Oh please! Will you marry me? I got sick and got this weird skin disease on my face. It's real hard to know what to do. Because I like some of those songs. It's such a weight to love David so much and so deep and true . . . and to have those songs in my heart and to, at the same time, know. Poor David. Albert Hall — we both did real good. Manchester — I cracked up and David helped me and rescued me with his tender and mighty love. I dreamed that night that I was told I had to go to Hell, and then write music that will bring people up from there. Things are getting clearer and clearer. I think I'm finally getting the idea. Last night while David was sleeping I poured out my heart to him and to the starry sky — I overflowed with an impassioned supplication that David's beautiful soul would be guarded and escorted for all eternity. Choirs of angels would refresh him while he sleeps with exquisite celestial music — these words fall sadly short of the feeling behind the supplication, just as my explanations of how much I love David always do. I wish he could see it always. (I worship you infinitely and love you just plain too . . .)*

David: *In the train (February 20) from Leeds to London drinking Courvoisier in coffee. Train compartments of worn sycamore panelling. White linen headrests. Alarm chain (penalty for improper use 25 pounds) Curtains you can pull right down & a little lamp blooms. Reading Harold Norse. Reading Jose Torres' book on Muhammed Ali. When I was at the top of my form; when Ali was Clay . . . Train passes cygnets on brimming canals. Norman Churches. 2 villagers in leather aprons & pudding-basin hair wave at the train. Stone fences overhill. Waterfalls over sluices. Tudor thatches a 2-barreled chimney laying threads of smoke over the lowlands. Plots of Brussels sprouts in backyards & we are pulling into what appears to be a bomb-damaged back end of London . . .*

Judee: *Last show: Oxford. David was wildly cheered again. I just returned to the Chelsea Cloister and David is out. I hope he is not getting drunk or carousing somewhere. I just did a radio interview and I told the whole truth. It was good. Most of it was about David and how great he is and how I worship and love him . . . I hope he comes home soon . . .*

David: *NOTES FOR LONDON POEM: The British walk by birds, — titwillows, thrushes, sparrows, vultures cruising, lovely doves & pigeons fly up and they flutter around . . . dogs with bushy ruffs, corgies in bowlers, edible chows (Chinese) with their blacks tongues, & there a greyhound, deep through the heart, is busking . . . A crowd passed over — a no-hoper from Stoke-Poges, meter maids, wankers, blokes, Irish hod carriers looking as if they're fixing to fight or cry hang out at The Rose Pub No. 86 Fulham Road, Fleet Street hacks, Wardour Street poetasters, charwomen . . . through these stiff lips pass much boiled meat; more per capita than is consumed anywhere else on earth, Judee tells me . . . Chop houses, Shepherd pie, gammon, tandooris, brie, steak & kidney puds, plaice & chips, scampi, trifle, Dover sole & Scotch salmon a delicacy. Smoking a crumbled Galoise in me curvilinear briar. Judee & me smoking "Parson's Pleasure" in the longstemmed churchwarden. Smoking a Player. Smoking opium. Smoking "cut golden bar" in the white clay pipe. Smoking a Rothman. Smoking too much, Judee. B.B.C. telly signs off too early. All night lorries rumble by on the wrong side of the street . . . & always out of the fog the small rain flecks down on cobblestone, on bobbies walking fuzz by fuzz, on the High Street, on Lord Nelson, Picadilly Circus, on David Bowie, on all the taxicabs with orange & blue lights, over Chelsea raining over Soho, Mayfair, over the County, over Abbey Road heath & moor over Stonehenge . . .*

Judee: *David is acting mad again. I worry about him. But our love is good. Something in his past makes him bitter.*

David: *In Soho, Lola and Trendy stroll by holding hands, or arm in arm. It is traditional for girls out walking to do that here. & in a darkened doorway a case of small lunar rocks; booty of a useless & expensive moon shot. They wear grotty built-up boots & pumps these days, reminiscent of Carmen Miranda & pachucos, but with weird bulbous toes; cartunes by Crumb or something out of a yellow submarine., Uglier the sex pygmy trendier the gear. Fuck it. The freckles, the vinegar, the useless plaint, all disease, all pigmentation which signifies, or used to, white man's human scenario, shows in these blighters like an orange icicle in a bank of snow & I say I'm one 1 to resemble these, but a son, with my secret name & yeah I am fair but ruddy, milk glass blushing with mad red wine . . . I like Judee's music. No, I love the music of Judee Sill. Shrill piping of a bird in a brush fire down where the San Fernando Valley is low . . . a little swallow, it has freed at last its wings from the thorns, & rises into blue sky, past the red tongues of the flames, through the cracking smoke, singing, clear into Heaven . . . Yeah Judee, I say I am a son, because I cannot bear to take the mark which keeps these motherfuckers sleepwalking & I can face a miracle I can see I am awake I have lost all companions & I still ache with love for them, miss them, & I can stand to strike out alone again & mine are the blues of one crucified & not the zeroic screams of ant baby . . .* (here a passage has been obliterated by a sepia magic marker)

BACK IN THE STATES

Judee: *A long time past and a lot has happened. David gone. He's coming back Sunday with dear James. I hope we can make it yet. Please. I have betrayed David and been untrue. I've caused him too much pain. I hope I can make it up to him. I must forgive David for not forgiving me. I'm the one that needs to be more forgiving. Today I got a letter from David, where he says he loves me still. I want so much to have "I" death so there will be room for Christ to enter. David is having a terrible time — he's taking downers and drinking a lot and he got in a fight with two guys and knocked one out, and he broke his leg in the same place again. I am quite weak with this lung infection and have to clean and prepare Rosehill House for David's and Jame's arrival. The house was bought last night. If their loan goes through, we should be out in a week with $5,000 or so. Please — let me be worthy of David's love, please let us grow from this purging . . .*

SONNET

O levy tributes to the votive girl
Who is your darling, welcome in your door
To that room's sill of knops & open flowers;
No stone is seen, of cedar is the floor . . .
Merciless cherubim lift gross veils curled
Thickly about one round hermetic hour . . .
To make her smile, attend her late & soon;
Bring as a gift your glimpse of morning light.
Adore her carefully as poets make —
Up carved, fantastic psalms to foil midnight
Crashing against the panes of a bright room
Full of quick dreams in which white angels flock . . .
      O levy tributes, while she smiles within,
      & all is cedar, & no stone is seen.

LIFT UP ON THE SILL

One night I was awake
beside you & you
had been farting in your nod
& it really stunk, honey.
& I laughed aloud because
it struck me so funny,
me cherishing you like I do
& you there at rest on smack
& percodans laying
silent but deadlines.
Well, I'd been opiated for some months
(longer if ya count the tack room),
& hadn't made love to you
in uh 3 months maybe honey
but I had a laugh,
& my adoration for your girl asleep
lit up my heart like a votive cup,
like it did just now
in Yolo County Hospital,
where She gives me a measly valium
& 3 darvons ever 4 hours.
But you're not here so I can't
caress your brown ass deeply
like I did
as our room guttered rosy candlelight
cut with the grayblue t.v. ray,
& the room redolent
of chili gone way wrong,
& Cal Worthington there every time
you tossed around,
desperate to sell a car
& a book about himself.
Wish you were beside me I'm lonely.
My legs are killing me.

4 January 1976

BEYOND THE SILL OF HOLLY

Okay sweetheart let's think of "them"
for a moment today of all days,
innocent & corrupt celebrating the birth of Jesus,
just think of the deals going down,
tormented & tormenting
ward heelers who imagine the ignoble
pain freezing their faces to be character,
pretty little girls opening bright packages, their smiles,
middle age arriving on time at the boyish stockbroker's
in the funny form of his new & almost
unnoticeably slacker muscle tone,
think of a weird star over a desert town
full of snoring jews
& maybe don't think about this now
but there are poor black karma suckers
out there reduced to worshipping hopelessness, —
things happening daily exactly as predicted
in the book of Revelations you know honey,
& think of something for us to say
to purveyors of *"Awake!"* & *"The Watchtower"*,
or to a gaggle of Hare Krishna retards about this.
I saw one loose guy, a wino I guess, yelling
at a last days street corner preacher:
"yeah yeah we know; so fucking what?"
That's what I'd say
except for Christmas Day,
thinking of Kid Manger far away
no crib for a bed,
but think of them out there
learning hardly anything is warm enough,
or stone hard or ice blue enough
for the iron circumstances around here,
& think of those getting their hearts broken
this moment for the first, worst time
by the sweetest thing down here, sweetheart,
then think of us.

Christmas Day 1975

DAVID DELIVERED
OUT OF MANY WATERS

Way down
beneath the ocean,
where I want to be,
past battered women in the tides,
shark & chum,
deeper than schools of bright wrasse,
clouds of blind ghost shrimp,
inking gray cerebral octopi,
I come climbing down
to find my stone baby boy
on his gone stone dolphin
riding

MY LAST DUTCHESS

She was a young Irish hot head rose.
A De Molay sweetheart in a brick tiara. —
"... *You were supposed to be real virtuous.*
If you did anything like with a boyfriend
you had to keep quiet about it."
So I married Barbara down in Vallejo.
Helge Stepanoff the Russian Finn was best man.
There was a fish & goose soirée afterwards.
Helge got quickly drunk & began to babble
nonsense to everyone, pleasantly.
Wild Al Russo was there in body.
He drank sullenly & watched Kim,
my child bride's handmaiden, —
bust her Japanese boyfriend's balls.
But since I had my dukedom got,
we danced our way out of that reception.
I drank my beer for a spell from a blue kitsch
goblet boosted as we waited for brunch
at the Madonna Inn.
We waltzed on the enormous tab
& had to push Barbara's oxide-orange
Volvo to escape.
To waltz is to leave without paying.
It was raining when we got home & rang the bell.
We stood in bed mostly. I loved her madly.
The Amazing Tramp took our calls,
explaining: *"They're in the annex, making it."*
Wild Al fell by going South, —
"I just can't stand this rainy winter,"
he explained.
It did rain continually there
in the dark forest by the river, —
but we didn't mind it at the time,
my child bride & my self, —
we kissed where the living rock is warm & dry.
& in the evenings we'd walk out
& stick these art-deco zircons & rhinestones
& diamonds on the covering nets of rain.

HE ROSE

Sexual bliss is torment with traction,
but I had lost a lot of traction
wandering around the frontyard
of my lady's cottage under the moon,
too tormented to enter too drunk
too soon since she laid my last pal
to rest
as I lay dying
through a jones in hospital . . .
Yeah, I was pitiful,
self pitifully drunk as the fool,
not a lord
with a kicking hard on
but no traction . . .
Drunken headlong
I fell into a bramble
whose active ingredients were:
roses, thorns, & dew.
Ice cold dew,
thorns like the last thoughts of Christ,
petals like lips of my lady.
I rose myself again
out of the bush in front of my lady's house
chilled & dignified,
sprinkled with stinging rubies,
crowned,
almost drowned,
I walked in carefully
so as not to lose
the kisses stuck to me,
the jewels the beauty marks
the tiny cherries & garnets of blood
the drops & rivulets of dew.

A LOVER'S PLEA

Just help me live undeceived
where the flying one
eternally dominates the crone,
or kiss my ass beneath a tree,
for I am sick of love.

A HAWK IN HYPERSPACE

for Loren Eiseley

A hawk flies freely in the sky.
With the very end of the eye he may be seen.

Into the sun he sometimes disappears,
but soon slides out again to glide,

a feathered wedge, down after-glints . . .
Against the thin translucent glass of china sky

climbs the white hot, helices from the dome,
again soars up, wider, in perfect turns,

exquisite as the quiet coils in clocks.
He's not re-entered from the sun!

When looked for now, point-blankness blinds
the eyes, then orange balls are floating

where he flew. The hawk is gone.
He swerved his finest line; —

Thin pinions traced the Möbius curve
& now he slips outside

along a convex bulge of the slick bubble-cup,
the Klein-blown blue.

HERS

Now God is still creating tygers,
which is righteous.
At another place on the spectrum
ducks are getting born,
which is as it should be.
But
when She wounds the tyger
in his sex,
or hangs great testicles
on a duck,
She's walking on the fighting side
of me.

When I would loiter tenderly
to ease her from a spit-hardened fort;
when I performed
antics of docked zeal
to try & melt her cold, cold heart,
ah, she seduced & double-crossed
behind such freakish wiles she had,
& in mine incredulity
grasped at my flame!
Adios thou cruel miss universe
ambiguous to see; —
you scheme a funeral of the name of the son
out in black torrents of wrongentity
which undermine all noble arrangements
though they shone bright as flame!

Wind down the war you.
& yeah, you can take back all
the organs I've repented of,
only hands off my pickle.
Get back out
the emergency exit
of the human construct,
bidizened in old
cloacas, dewlaps,
hobnailed kidneys

& liver . . .
who knows what all
only leave me alone.

Just a minute.
You can take with you
all these sleepwalking
motherfuckers whom
softly & tenderly
& over a period of time
commit cold blooded
murder

NAMOR

Hour before dawn
when cities bottom
on black sand, —
a man is coughing,
little girls dream of primal hair . . .
A boy is wandering
lost by a howling sea
in a daybreaking red like old blood
horrendous on slick tide rocks
stuck with crown-of-thorns starfish
& anemones sprung open all the way, —
cunts full of poison jewels . . .
surf breaks cold incarnadine
around his knees . . .
He is a loss, or Hero,
somber after his night encounter:
like an ancient & sinister memory
he saw shuffled into the dark strand
the pale flat sting ray
whose rusty spine stuck antenna-like
out of the shallow waves
to broadcast unbearable imaginings;
death under alien moonlight, —
ankle & achilles gnawed in the tide rocks,
upturned face caught wide
open in the razors of the blue rays . . .
starry anemones shriveled brown
in that light's bale
& fell into the sea
before he freed his narrow foot
& limped on wearily
by the ribbed side of a savage mare
homeward

toward the gold day

vanishing

A JOVIAN TRAVELER
or, Mirth Over Brine

Being

A POEM IN A HIGH MANNER
BY ONE WHO TRAVELED IN ROSE RED MARS
A MASTERMINDED HIS OWN CRUCIFIXION THERE
IN ORDER THAT HIS SOUL
MIGHT HEAD FOR THE HEART OF THE SUN
NEVERMINDING THE CHEAP BLONDE FURNITURE
OF EARTH, OR THOSE HOLLYWOOD BEDS
OF THE FIXED STARS...

Live as a kind
somnambulist,
or a voyeur on the heights
of Hel. Live well, —
nod in Gethsemane . . .
Everything's His double
cross
where nothing measures up, —
Jesus' last epiphany!
Rich guys have no religion.
Punks have no future.
The Elect are subject to show
up in striking black livery
with white piping.
You watch.
Angels dance on pinheads.
Camel pureé squirts through
the eye of the needle.
Live out your retirement
into deeper exiles still . . .

I set fire to bitter walking papers.*
I was ever the I am not in those good days
Kid Thunderhead swapped with the rose.
I never made the world, — not clocks,
not waves, — nor aspired to find

my cameo crushed into awned wheat.
After so much loss
in places I couldn't even make it to,
I got behind my absence
with hardly a shortcoming lost, —
just in a peter of salt dissolving
in a cup of winter water.
So the drifter muses: if he came alive
in time, staving the distance in,
would he return to where his tears welled up,
waste again his fix of identity,
say his so longs again, & leave?

It was my hair
standing on end . . . no, relaxing,
as sudden thoughts rise & set,
as the town is afraid of its own shadow,
as nose picking is always a sign
of a profound spiritual malaise,
O madly hopeful fool!
If one is dirty
tricked, or blessed in space
in which one's body walks
nor rots nor thrives
but knows when Pole star
flares rosy in soul
as blood clouds a tumbler
of winter water,
what the Hel?
A riddle mad
a poem made
against all flags,
as long pale feet in sky blue boots
step down from Heaven . . .
& O you insectile ones

in your jumpsuits & goggles, —
the mad smiles of the Gods
torment all comers!
So many white flags whipped & snapping
in this nuclear haboob . . !
Japanese banner the finest:
rising sun shining
like a red rubber ball!

Perhaps alone shall I?
When I do finally kak,
you know I'm gonna cut the Devil
dead. Then at the Mother
of pearly gates I'm gonna ask
all these celestial guardians
"Y' all wanna do this fair,
one angel at a time?"
Then dance my way
through circuits & throngs
swinging this razor here
slinging feathers
& sky blue blood ever where
'til I've won my way
up to the Book
wherein I'm gonna write
my true & full name:
David Omer Bearden
'buked & scorned
by every God damned low down
boar on several cold stars
you can see from here,
& by that gamy auxiliary
of clubby razors & bitch
marmosets back on Earth . . !

. . . The mummer walks.
In the stares & songs he'll ever be.
But there are leaving wheels
that roll up & fly off the paucity
of your conceptual depth,

terrestrial marionettes!
You yield what one might call
leaving power . . . give anti-gravity, —
headed out in mine now . . .
as everything you've got recedes
into the past
at the speed of the light
in my eyes.

Appendix B

CLEANING UP TOMBSTONE

"A cowboy from New Mexico rode into Tombstone on a fine horse, stabled it at the O.K. Corral, then went broke and offered the animal for sale at a bargain price. The buyer who grabbed the opportunity paid up and asked about the ownership title. The cowboy responded, 'The title is good as long as you go west with him, but don't take him east; it is not so good in that direction,'"

— *Paul Mitchell Marks,*
AND DIE IN THE WEST

Alkali face of freezer burn
to a dimpled horizon
of moribund white baby flesh.

Long slits of arroyos
scar the far hard pan
tufted with dead black armpit hair.

Volcanic chimneys
jut from mean drifts
like tusks black from sucking sugar.

This stunned wide
sky regarding countenance
is traversed fitfully
& scuffed by thin dust devils
of yesteryear.

In this La Mancha
they often hanged a boy
for something his father made him do

while through rough blue
clouds to the north
he flew up into the sunlight
playing over the game.

That lynched kid
had been starved
down to stealing
good men's horses for meat.

Johnny-Behind-the-Deuce
threw down on him
in his camp on the picket wire
as the kid bled a little
                salamander
into the wild
roses & lilies,
listening to the voice
crying in that desert
beneath a sky-litmus wig
redder for what happened there.

Bauxite, permanganate & borax
under Jupiter Pluvius.
Radio waves carry
Pedro Infante
& The Mighty Clouds of Joy
over Del Rio
swaying in the wind
with the stars.

Outside Blythe,
titanic figures of a human being
& of an unknown animal
keep silent watch in the desert
through moonburn & rainlight.

Rain,
& hard winds on the mesa,
loosen that kid from the minerals
of illusion locked dry,

& interpolate him into here,
flash-drowning world
one moment
before the blink.

SUBMARINER

Even as gold
salts arriving
dry behind the eyes
& wheat in the shock
on Ophir's fields
he would dream in the nights
off goat rock
of running down
canals at the bottom
of the starry waters . . .
all musics this trimmed hush
as the currents
rushing carried him . . .
& now he is running away, —
see where his fire glints in the mere!
Upon land, blonde soprano
of the horned Wagnerian lady is
winnowing hamstrung vainglory
over a had battlefield
where dogged butchers
under Major Kirk
took the anthill!
So smuggle silk to Babylon,
but I must tell you
he is running away
from the courts
martial of that world, —
on the lam from its very
household dogknot, —
glancing way down into the sky
of his watery midnight's
silvery pepper of galaxies . . !

O I know
silver was nothing accounted of
in the days of Solomon,
but Ophir certain existed
& will perhaps be glimpsed again
when at last the butchers step out
& the stars say to Man go!

David Bearden, Oklahoma City, 1960. Summer break from Tulsa University.

SO LONG AT THE FAIR, &
DOWN AT THE PALOMINO CLUB

"carry me along, taddy,
like you done through the toy fair"
     — James Joyce

Hell we figured It would get behind
the food-exhibits, the hog-judging, etc.,
but Christ, toward late afternoon a body
couldn't he'p but notice Its dense soul-lessness;
Its implacable refusal to go along with our
recreation, —
We all laughed to scorn those old Zeppelin
dinosaurs you know,
& winked about the Toad-in-a-Hole,
& that cotton-candy teenage Tiresias;
we dug those glib barkers that cut up
fruits & vegetables, —
our gang bush-wacked a clown with water pistols
fulla tears, pecked paranoid turkey-dick
til its comb got red,
slapped it on the feather
with a generous *"right-on, buddy,"*
& jest righteously kept on trucking
toward total fun . . .
Pervo kept asking *"do we love one another?"*,
Spanky warned It how we never-mind this fly-ash
we breathe now
unless some bummer's sob
or hawk & spit brings it up,
threatening to bring our party down;
then black flack flowers burst
into bloom around pigasus,
bloody that face of wood-pulp & bat-shet
whining about how it hurts to sober-up . . !
(It'll tell ya anything out front,
but when you go in you're more'n likely to find
auld sweinhund ripe for the Home . . !)
So anyway we split the pleasure-fair's
barbarous parade, where to see what we like to do
is proof of Its fault-line,

& on Highway 1, as the switchophrenic welcher
cried *"I love you"*, we ate Its stare
(of blue pork eye of brown) down both barrels;
loyally the little woman backed her man up
in this . . . Lastly, down in the Palomino Club
while that beautiful freak goddaughter
of Kitty wells wailed,
our compassion all puked away, we toasted
Its death in a double-black rush,
smiling, & handed Its snout the glass,
conjuring our Man right-on over to the high-side,
in the rite   in the right   on the right
  in the *"Love? . . . Self-betrayal"*   in the Wright
    O my brothers   inn our   own   right in
      the right   what was it the old
        draB fo novA said about
          It's alright   ?   in the right
             in the ride
      rose-hips   vit   am   ins
         the right
           Way

Los Angeles County Fair
& The Linda Ronstadt Set
September 1972

IN A STAR CHAMBER

'Twas the night before Christmas, —
EarthMother & the Final Solution
were appearing at Playland;
Aldous Presley was agonizing
in the rock garden, —
great gray screamers blocked
the fire escape . . .
all was lost Enola Gay.
Me & Louie burglarized thunderheads
blew feathers.
(When riming continues
to such an extent
the original crystal is unrecognizable
or nearly so,
the resulting snow is called grauple.
Much rain
is melted grauple . . .)
When the nuclear haboob calms,
comes the cold rain
to settle blown word dust . . . sorry
the Kid caused you to know
hate & sorrow. Man!

lying on the shopfloor
at Westinghouse
the day the last bolt
was ceremonially fitted,
with Einstein visibly present,
Wichita, Kansas.

DIRT TRACK ELIMINATIONS

The old crowd has prettily nearly discorporated;
    Gene Andreau is still wintering in Helsinki,
Peri, little Peri the manatee, seem like just
    another hole in the ocean,
The Kid lost the Quality contest, & is now
    indolently supported by angels,
La Infanta was finally made a civil servant
    by order of the junta
    with certification *"super numerary"*,
Both the Partisans & the Man still refuse to
    mad ape goner the secular miracle
    of their communion,
Shakey Will had his plays to get called in
    for pulping, & his ghost to get laid
    in an alley posted with psychedelic bills,
A heavy left fielder was quite present at Golgotha
    for his routine political execution,
Tarry McCull & his privates
    jam nightly down on the lower west side,
Nedra Eb wails to standing room only
    near the station.
    The Drifter did escape.
During a good will inspection tour of his
    stockyards, Penrod Farmal
    was inadvertently smothered in a bucolic
    end product,
Dave has paid down on his own modest bungalow
    right outside the village of Doughty-At-Bay,
    where he likes to listen to the old timers
        talk about the end
            of this whole world.

FORTE PIANO

Quieter & quieter the Planets
the Sioux, trees, nightingales, apes,
fresco Gods in the dome, & many others . . .

Loudly burn the Stars, the Sons,
poppies in noon, the buzzing flies
in their throes . . .

POOR BASTARDS

for the dignity of Joe Cocker

I'm nearly through, —
the day is overchased,
the sky is true.
On radio some exotic form
of erotic quality contest
fumes & teems with wired announcers
for the afternoon of the fond . . .

& the Dodgers' half game lead
leaves me rather indifferent,
know what I mean?
Do you watch empty V?
Packing radio ears?
Are you Pac-man?
Now you must eat your steady girl.

Grime of centuries
he called me apocalypse rose
or roach. & you serve
quit claim deeds in his service.
But O cruel soldiers of the bull,
you may yet star me on the gospel plow
when I sign off the air
& auger in to the Western Lands.

Outskirts of Saturn Street blew dust
through home box,
hard hearts hardening
against upcoming colderness
leaching milk of the fields . . .

Red door closing black in radio silence
leaving not a thin line
of taut light beneath —
but hold . . . Brothers, remember
when I fastened the ratty boa
around the neck of Tuffy, the family spaniel,
& we all laughed?

Breaker breaker forget it, —
but David Omer here paying
to muster out,
& go ponder that in a clean outbuilding.
See the inexorably gentle white
probe light meant to impart
how green we marched
to this place known as stony cross.

Rooster tail of blood
off leaving wheel,
fireball of re-entry.
& just as he moved
to douse the light
a poor gray moth blew in
& kissed himself
all over the bright wall.

NORTHERN MAYAN LIGHTS
ON SEATTLE

They say enlightenment is the truth
taking the place of the dream,
but I've always had a very active
imagination, out here in the cold.
One of my escaping dreams has me
calmly, if a little drunkenly moving around
an apartment in a northern city
with Grieg softly swirling around the radio
& winter coming in from the sea.

The sky outside is bruise blue
& moiling agony peach, —
shafts of silver strike the sound.

The streets are wet & shiny.
People hurry along in expensive raincoats
or under umbrellas. City people, —
you know, those beautiful slickers
much handsomer than one's self,
square hairlines, flat waists,
firm lines in muted tasteful clothes
hurrying to offices to pubs
of panelling & yellow lamps,
to calm women with smug little smiles
& shining coifs & eyes . . .

Bums vaguely grab at my arm
as I hasten past with my package
to my rooms in this dream.
& here I am.

SHEERNESS AS SEEN THROUGH THE NORE

ἔριφος ἐς γάλ' ἔπετου
(A kid, I fell into milk.)
    ORPHIC FORMULA.

        The Cardinal came through
    the operation at Rip Van Winkle municipal
  hospital / Dorothy Kilgallen did not.
   Seemingly inconsequential
 as death throes of the cherubin,
little gasps are incessantly escaping
through the sea of lips.
         So that the air grows
    momentarily moist . . . but Lo! One mouth
  is closing in eternal sleep, amidst the
 long rotation. Extremities grow chill
in any case. & they will perform their
vivisection. So that lungs are subsequently
shown to be stained always a bitter brown-black,
     while they find pale stones
    like jawbreakers & dwarf moons
   have clogged the long bones
  & flawed the liver. Pass on then,
as through milk darkly,
 in a surf of breathing lips,
  as if cadaver were typical
   of this long rotation,
     this ocean of heaving mouths,
this humid, bloody air!

SNOW'S CHOWDER

for Konrad Lorenz

Walking alone down the rivertown
in a wanton soup of the evening,
beautiful soup stirred by biker's far
chopper snarl in its black humours,
a cold going aspirin of near full moon
over the crenellated watch towers,
me under the gun . . .
I pass some raggedy Christers
loitering in front of the Russian River
Christian Center across the way, —
a guy in a burnoose is whirling in circles.
One of their females is lovely
as a belly dancer . . .
"Evening, friends," I say.
"Jesus loves you!" their charismatic
leader replies . . .
I walk on to my room
wet with that one ton soup.
I'm carrying my brown bag
from Guerneville liquors & grocery
containing a pint of Royal Gate Vodka,
32 fl. oz. of orange juice,
a small box of Ritz crackers, —
all to put together with this
can of Snow's Chowder,
& the absence
of certain bitches & sons of
in this my *"studio"*, —
in order to stew quietly in the oblivion
roiled with hours
of a night on my days off . . .
Lighting my little oil lamp
I mix hot milk & potatoes & clams . . .

Jesus it tasted good,
drunk as I got!
… & I glimpsed Charles Bukowski paddling
Bob Dylan's fanny in the waterpearl
as I fell
asleep through kerosene-lit
dervishes & houris.

HIS

"smoking euphemisms karmic hoboing wing"
— David Moe

a harml
an impotent fat guy phoned flabby stud an ass-kicking!
flab stud a weatherman in mary van dyke show!
only the volte face flab stud
he flabbergasted het up marmosets into conniving
huddles flabby stud did & fucked huggie boy 2
had a big wrong body on him
flabby stud in his cups dug state of bustitude
sho like his gloomy fun ol flabby stud
him very white danger guy
he gods mug shot
flabby stud seas hells & stairwells
he stares well
purple girl with *"aboriginal mind"* ya love to hate?
had one hard bitten main: flabby stud
stoned as a fucking tree
not walking but soughing   lame but great so flabby
stud palms it   man
                              rip torn
off as
juvenalia!   big
        bum   bob mitchum

SOMBER SYSTEM*

by Pablo Neruda
translated by David Bearden
Santa Barbara County Jail

From every one of these days black as old irons,
& opened by the sun like big red oxen,
& barely sustained by the air & by dreams,
& gone suddenly & without remedy,
nothing has made up for my tormented origins,
& the imbalanced measures that circulate in my heart
are forged there by day & night, in solitary,
& hold disheveled & sad quantities.

Thus then, like a vigilante gone insensible & blind,
incredulous & condemned to a doleful spying,
facing the wall where every day of time becomes one,
my various faces gather & form chains
like huge flowers pallid & heavy,
tenaciously replaced & defunct.

* Appendix C

BLOOD MERIDIAN
or, The Evening Redness in the West

A Ballad

Farewell my portrait of the Prima Vera,
goodbye my smoky star,
adios indelible picture
so long my heart's desire.

For the mirror empties into morning,
& the clouds leak glittering snow,
& the dark bright light torments me,
as the sun is sinking low.

Yes the sky tortures me sweetly
as the cows are walking home,
& the swallows are returning,
& arrives the fiery gloam.

No woman can release me
so my shiny craft can leave,
& the gnarled moon ignores me
as they're bringing in the sheaves.

O leafy path through the Prima Vera
beneath a high green star,
be quenched in oblivious music,
so long my lute and lyre.

BOUQUET OF BONE

for Florida's electric chair

Couple of boys
tortured a girl to death
at a swimming party
in the thrill of holding forth
the vicious rose's torn red dress.
Today they fry
while sitting in a chair.
Society's unwobbling pivot
just in spades,
removes them to where
boys & girls cannot be
pardoned from,
or exiled from.
Where water, air & earth
jolt away in hideous fire.

… While the blue sheep feed
close by the hermitage.

French poet Arthur Rimbaud

THE MAN WHO FELL TO EARTH

"The Putrefaction of the philosophers
is a moistening of dry bodies, that they may
be restored to their former state of Greening
and Growing."
    — Trismosin

1.

shut the little window up
   charred rose inner walls
      make me a pallet on the floor
         for it is time for me to slide
            broken filament
      jerk the wires
take off livery
       adios kid
   more adamantly sweet than life
     the high sheriff
        of that living which is possible
is vivisecting you
            sipping bitter funeral beer
       pale house scares the child
    mulled hair
    face fond & mad
to dance, to sing, to play the guitar
      with Jovial bone
  forever widening in the warm glimmer
        of a new breath
     where the ragged rose lips
      kiss eternity's sunrise
   fondle the rugose sac
       limbs roast in their sleeves
     torture growth
    outside mists fall. children hurry on.
       whine & bark
     remember & mourn
   Nihil dicit
       this is no song
         bowels moving in fear
      & sorrow

in outer dark
a dog lifts
his foot of void
what is there to know?
outside in the winds
beautiful voices forgetting
words inflected by fresh rose lips
light & whistles
laughter
outside lips chap. toes chill in little
shoes
etiolate rose
in a bell jar
you will never go out again?

2.

as the heart froze
the hand slowed
the face returned
the stare of spilth
on sidewalks.
brain meat set
mind went shocked
by what it had forgot
& the dark side of the eyeballs read dim charts:

"despair pours over the heart
like liquid air
but that pump-head will pump alright
though any colder
must shatter the brain . . ."
& both had broken in the thaw.
hand touched the face
& it was drifting sand.
ears winced at sirens
& whining dogs.
mind squeaked with memory
the heart was scaling down
to no priestholes in the house . . .
O outlaw Art

Rimbaud was no earth householder, —
      got no ennabling act passed . . .
        let pitiful Satan bequeath
    to the boys in the slot trenches
the balm of his unearthly
                resignation . . .
& a voice's diagram issued around the tongue:

"Give me a World. As streets mash back,
      as belly-rolls will lip a flimsy shirt.
Give me it! It is my dynamite!
        as the thin edges of the ocean flap!
I'll take it like iron on slate & crack,
      as the mind rises through the spine like sap!
Give me my World like hot white fish to eat . . ."

              . . . slowly bricks became meat
          even to enlarged pores
        along the curbs . . .

3.

Planets blind in frozen shadows of Monoceros
      purify my heart
Great ocean weeping beyond joy & grief to the weird daytime moon
      purify my heart
Space of wounded galaxies spattered with milk of Kali-Ma
      purify my heart
Stars aborning of falling sand burning to a heart of glass
      purify my heart
Mexican boy who bloodied my nose & we both were horrified
      purify my heart
Birds singing in the ruins of my boyhood home
      purify my heart
O Milky Way which flows in eyes of Woman
      purify my heart
Grave waiting for this body somewhere
        under cottonwoods or a ditch by barrel-fires
      purify my heart
Love failing as soul takes off for void
      purify my heart

Old negress fallen on the sidewalk crying with no sound
   purify my heart
Young bodies fucking with love in the park in study hall
   purify my heart
Poor feet aching in their graves of shoes
   purify my heart
Mother neglected in your house of woe
   pray, purify my heart
Death with the noseless face the vacant home
   purify our living hearts
Knights templars O lion-hearted Man
   purify my heart
Soft belly! Twisted hate rolls of alabaster fat
   killing my Manly joy
   purify my heart
Friend gone who forgot all my soul when vengeance bought you
   purify my heart
O "Character" O "Personality" lascinated overshrill
   purify my heart
Jesus who bled my ego's agonized blood on Calvary
   forgive, purify my heart
Litany begging for mad space of my desire, O supplication
   please purify my heart
Clothes of Americans poor poor freak or straight
   exiled in streets
   purify, purify
Fried meat of everyday this mouth opened in Hades for its supper
   purify my heart
Body I torture like a bad boy a toad
   purify my heart
Heart heart O aching heart of panic blood
   purify our hearts

THE SAUCERS ARE LATE

Fermi's Question,
& a Zoo Hypothesis

Nuclear winter
& it is still
news how blue violets are
out where the garden gate is slamming
incessantly in the rain
storm scrubbing wormwood

'Til all its armatures dwine bone
into depths of a far refrigerator
where a banana blackens
the mind of an odd man gone
out in a stunning explosion of snow
near the sea

A roiled river
widens & grows slow
then it is still, save for Theramin music
down empty streets of Scarsdale
where the enemy sends a mosquito
& the smoky night goes up in sleep.

LA LLORONA

streets of Juarez

From sodium vapor suns
ticked off moths fall away
into the pit on the street

One day it was o'er
that storm in a bug
begging on wall street

Above the water palaces
a wise star is bleeding fire
like a wound in the eastern sky

A female voice wails in the night
"O my children, you are lost,
where shall I hide you?"

AMAZING GRACE

—from somewhere else invisible & congruent

in the deep of the hellish tellurian
pecking order,
what last lambent home welcomes & warms to
the groaning traveler,
allays his freezing age,
his aching heart
refused by every fellow
hideous human angel
the miracle of the secular communion?

angel banned
rose from out the abyss
of excluded middles?
one of those wayward pilgrims
picked up walking
too far from Portland

to have a known destination?

NORTHSTAR

for Janine Pommy-Vega

O why go limping over the earth?
I'm living on Midway Road, who'd say
darkly, my star smouldering in a dream,
like a lodestone in the sky?
Who'd say, over the phone, in a nightmare,
& how could a wrong number reach me
on an old party line?
I'm not on the line.
But please make something warm
like morning's passage looking down
on me, — into the slants & rises
where red & white roses shone
like a gallant & humorous mistake,
as I have made it home, —
this gnostic with lover's nuts
to live in the colors of the Lord,
just like I never could before,
down Midway Road, outside the town,
in a shelter break of eucalypti
molting their barks in scrolls!
I take some lone rides, do you Janine?
Like Highway 37 down to Marin County,
past Mare Island, Valley of the Moon . . .
A lighter fluid
sworls peacock eyes
in slack banks & flat bodies of water . . .
pale jade fire reeds
crush beneath icy winds
on electric blue sloughs . . .
Titan Kachina skeletons
stride far away over tide flats into haze
in the last days
high wires singing thin
white heron
              on one leg all day . . .

But I come home with El Greco in my hands.
So serve my heart back
Western style: obviously burnt,
but rare at the center.
& bring me my blue Marine
Band harp of beaten tin; —
I want to blow Amazing
Grace real soulfully
to these shaggy eucalypti soughing
around my home...
for I am back breathing
warm like stone fresh
from the fire bath.
Christ risen sends me.
O why go limping over the earth?
I am living on Midway Road,
& who'd say he has seen
a star smouldering in a vacant lot, —
in the darkness of old mammalian politics,
in the darkness of human slot bardo,
as if calumny were a song?
O please lady let me make you
warm, as when my morning light
looked out from where the roses look,
& who sends you?

Wichitan poet Alan Russo

SEE THE ELEPHANT

"with fragments of the great unwonderable thrown in"
— *Alan Russo*

See eidetic poikilothermism
through a fused stained rock candy window,
see a buggy rose bush with a burning turk inside,
see his fingers of rose marble
fret the blue axe,
see milklines in the kid
seeing potato love in delirious professions,
see what a baby sees,
see a new love letter in the shetter,
see the beast's one-sided push
wear out hot miscreants,
see a creature on the cusp
of the big pink man & the thin blue partisans
struggle his human wings,
see the demons with human tendencies,
see the cards, & how one bets it all,
see blanched silverbacks, in clouds of buzzing flies,
sacrifice pigeons & calves,
see the incendiary gnash his teeth
famished for calm sleep,
see Mom thrilled, eager for details,
see a walker disappear through the door & burn,
see the burnt not doing well on the circuit,
see the giddy line midway
where currents of the sea pull hair,
see long pale feet of Jesus Christ
walking in whitecaps on the spatial void,
see the Weird of the Wanderer,
see a fever we deem thieves' delight,
see who can See, & who can Not,
see Christ only alive in the walking still,
finally see Hölderlin's carpenter
in each & every friend,
see the Love, see the Hate,
see the fire from within,
see the fatally crushable rose,

see mandala centers vaporize
that seemed harder than the hubs of Hell,
see St. George & the word tape worm,
come, & see
      deadpan A#1, he's seen the elephant,
see old impossibly mundane karma
involving doughnut waitresses,
see, through the rosace in a star chamber,
the baby's breath taken over
by the spreading dog bane,
the rank arrow-weeds,
the flowering judas,
the charred white apocatastatic rose
beneath a sky of bright demento blue,
see a Hell whole of a lot in Heaven,
see a clear round silvering wheel
dart, hover, & leave up sky,
see the great unwonderable…

Where is it now?
Out in the glowing winds.
What left it out there?
My lord of karma, & my family…
What hurt it so?
My sister's sorrow was the worst to bear…
Where will it go?
It will disappear in air…

THE WIDENING HOME
or, Rage Over A Lost Penny

*"... marveling that the sky
had brought forth a certain
new phenomenon to be compared
with the other stars,
immediately I got ready my instrument."*
— Tycho Brahe

With a skyward telemetric glance
the night man at Mount Airy
noted the Vargula Nebula
looking oddly luminous tonight.

Jumped in a car
& headed home.
Ground fog in low places
stirred beside the highway.
Down bars & bar ditches trash did blow.

Inside a blue Volkswagen rabbit
remnants of wind & Beethoven,
moonlit & snotty.

Past darkened warrens & sites
where beings caught for an aquarium
slept through their rest
as a mag 5 object passed
unnoticed at the wheel

above it all,
stars popped like Mayan corn,
& a bone moon shone
& grinned, & whistled Dixie.

Tulúm, Quintana Roo, Mexico

REDRESS
AT THE TEMPLE
OF THE DIVING GOD

1.

On the train going south
through Mexico
we lay in a heavenly *camarín*,
my child bride & myself,
& during the night the train would stop
in the jungle, & we'd walk out
into the chirring of the stars
peering & smiling into faces
of Mayan conductors
& solid brakemen swinging lanterns
& we'd smile & strain to understand
their beautiful lingo
& buy plates of *machaca* & tomatoes
& drink beer with folks in white pajamas
& be very happy.
But O baby Jesus walking
the princess of Anadarko send me now, —
Bill Holden was a tough man
Natalie Wood was a fox
indecent Doris is the apocalypse spud
& I am Homer on the sea...

There was a showdown long ago.
He struck one of those
phosphor matches on his teeth
or was it down the fly of his Levi's? —
We stood there in the West
in the weird white sagebrush face to face
like planets. I rolled my own too,
slow like him
under the busted clabber of the moon, —
mighty herds of thunderheads stampeding . . .
the wind kept bending his sombrero back, —
when clouds tore in that light

eyes were conchos or pearl rattlers.
A long time we stood there.
Maybe we've stood there forever
in a moonlit circle. Or one man falls
down, his coffin nail real
slowly coming apart on his face.

2.

for Neal Cassady,
   Genie of the Fireball Mail

They shone for me
as the appearance of the bow
that is in the cloud
in the day of rain, —
his rough lights wherein now
I am caused to see
a tiny hawk high overhead
the hummingbird wizard
on the left of the red rose
near a dreaming
yellow velvet ant walking
across some dust beneath
a sonny & balneal Genie
whom I was made to witness hop along
in a quicklime light & harsh winds
shaking the darling buds of May's
gamy marmoset vestals,
cruel sergeants at arms
& priests of Mandrill Rock, —
Chacma *chacs* trehala hawks alula *Ha!*
(fascists did quail
before his heart attack)
— after Kid Free's tongue,
human outlawry, —
400 rabbits . . !
All in mirror of beryl
& the grieving thorn
I map & sing you these brain-ends, —
& tie them into the shock

while fixed stars above the abyss
wink in the smoking night mirror
at me, or the near sun glares.
From dense jungle under *Jupiter Pluvius*,
from the afterburner of reality,
from the radio sky, from nowhere,
from Hell, I made the flowery war
on meaninglessness, —
wayward Babe from head to toe!
What was spirit of Man
peregrine
beyond the pale
fine ash
fair but ruddy
as red heels of the old regime,
new born baby man.
Flesh fresh old angel hair
bright Christmas tree of nerves
in milkglass flushed
with the last red wine
of an inferior race from all time
so that the likeness of the firmament
upon the heads of the living creature
was as the color of the terrible crystal
stretched forth over their heads above
leaving the bank
of the body
holding his stream & grounds…
Man came out ape late
& saw an outlaw drifter from the east
of Mars, whose eyes shone dark bright
there were appearance glows in smoke
like coals of living fire . . .
So that assassin flayed him,
breast cutter tore his heart
up by the root
& that without remedy
O Father God
so that blown out he finishes
circuit of his walkabout amazed, —
while animal crackers in his traces broke

over the horizon levin shone
wind quickened silver & he rose
freed scintilla glancing down
rifled trunks of his heart raised high
opened up, emptied, spattered the lost face
(& dark eyes & thirsty deadpans of your priests)
in rain water mingled with blood
singing plumed tongue of pain
over the rainbow, through the blue light
over Maya ruins of teeth
over the gem stone star
of our concern

rolling

Tulúm, Quintana Roo, Mexico —
Night desk, Mount Airy,
Pennsylvania, 1987

Coda

LEAVING WHEELS

The mummer walks, —
in the stares & songs he'll ever be.
But there are leaving wheels
that roll up & fly off
the paucity of your conceptual depth,
terrestrial marionettes!
You yield what one might call
leaving power . . . give anti-gravity, —
headed out in mine now . . .

as everything he's got recedes
into the past
at the speed of the light
in our eyes.

1 March 1976

HONTE

Tant que la lame n'aura
Pas coupé cette cervelle,
Ce paquet blanc, vert et gras,
A vapeur jamais nouvelle,

(Ah! Lui, devrait couper son
Nez, sa lèvre, ses oreilles,
Son ventre! et faire abandon
De ses jambes! ô merveille!)

Mais, non; vrai, je crois que tant
Que pour sa tête la lame,
Que les cailloux pour son flanc,
Que pour ses boyaux la flamme,

N'auront pas agi, l'enfant
Gêneur, la si sotte bête,
Ne doit cesser un instant
De ruser et d'être traître,

Comme un chat des Monts-Rocheux,
D'empuantir toutes sphères!
Qu'à sa mort pourtant, ô mon Dieu!
S'élève quelque prière!

— Arthur Rimbaud

Appendix B

ADIOSES

Yo no encedí sino un papel amargo.

Yo no fui causa de aquel Buenos Días
que se dieron el trueno con la rosa.

Yo no hice el mundo, no hice los relojes,
no hice las olas ni tampoco espero
hallar en las espigas mi retrato.

Y de tanto perder donde no estuve
fui quedándome ausente
sin derrochar ninguna preferencia
sino un monte de sal desmoronado
por una copa de agua del invierno.

Se pregunta el viajero si sostuvo
el tiempo, andando contra la distancia,
y vuelve adonde comenzó a llorar:
vuelve a gastar su dosis de yo mismo,
vuelve a irse con todos sus adioses.

— Pablo Neruda

SISTEMA SOMBRIO

De cada uno de estos días negros como viejos hierros,
y abiertos por el sol como grandes bueyes rojos,
y apenas sostenidos por el aire y por los sueños,
y desaparecidos irremediablemente y de pronto,
nada ha substituido mis perturbados orígenes,
y las desiguales medidas que circulan en mi corazón
allí se fraguan de día y de noche, solitariamente,
y abarcan desordenadas y tristes cantidades.

Así, pues, como un vigía tornado insensible y ciego,
incrédulo y condenado a un doloroso acecho,
frente a la pared en que cada día del tiempo se une,
mis rostros diferentes se arriman y encadenan
como grandes flores pálidas y pesadas
tenazmente substituidas y difuntas.

— *Pablo Neruda*

Appendix D

THE MENTAL TRAVELLER

I travel'd thro' a Land of Men,
A Land of Men & Women too,
And heard & saw such dreadful things
As cold Earth wanderers never knew.

For there the Babe is born in joy
That was begotten in dire woe;
Just as we Reap in joy the fruit
Which we in bitter tears did Sow.

And if the Babe is born a Boy
He's given to a Woman Old,
Who nails him down upon a rock,
Catches his Shrieks in Cups of gold.

She binds iron thorns with around his head,
She pierces both his hands & feet,
She cuts his heart out at his side
To make it feel both cold & heat.

Her fingers number every Nerve,
Just as a Miser counts his gold;
She lives upon his shrieks & cries,
And She grows young as he grows old.

Till he becomes a bleeding youth,
And She becomes a Virgin bright;
Then he rends up his Manacles
And binds her down for his delight.

He plants himself in all her Nerves,
Just as a Husbandman his mould;
And She becomes his dwelling place
And Garden fruitful Seventy fold.

An aged Shadow, soon he fades,
Wand'ring round an Earthly Cot,
Full filled all with gems & gold
Which he by industry had got.

And these are the gems of the Human Soul,
The rubies & pearls of a lovesick eye,
The countless gold of the akeing heart,
The martyr's groan & the lover's sigh.

They are his meat, they are his drink;
He feeds the Beggar & the Poor
And the wayfaring traveller:
For ever open is his door.

His grief is their eternal joy;
They make the roofs & walls to ring;
Till from the fire on the hearth
A little Female Babe does spring.

And she is all of solid Fire
And gems & gold, that none his hand
Dares to stretch to touch her Baby form,
Or wrap her in his swaddling-band.

But She comes to the Man she loves,
If young or old or rich or poor;
They soon drive out the aged Host,
A Beggar at anothers door.

He wanders weeping far away,
Until some other take him in;
Oft blind & age-bent sore distrest,
Until he can a Maiden win.

And to allay his freezing Age
The Poor Man takes her in his arms;
The Cottage fades before his sight,
The Garden & its lovly Charms.

The Guests are scatter'd thro' the land,
For the Eye altering alters all;
The Senses will themselves in fear,
And the flat Earth becomes a Ball;

The stars, sun, moon, all shrink away,
A desart vast without a bound,
And nothing left to eat or drink,
And a dark desart all around.

The honey of her Infant lips,
The bread & wine of her sweet smile,
The wild game of her roving Eye,
Does him to Infancy beguile:

For as he eats & drinks he grows
Younger & younger every day;
And on the desart wild they both
Wander in terror & dismay.

Like the wild Stag she flees away,
Her fear plants many a thicket wild;
While he pursues her night & day,
By various arts of Love beguil'd,

By various arts of Love & Hate,
Till the wide desart planted o'er
With Labyrinths of wayward Love,
Where roams the Lion, Wolf & Boar,

Till he becomes a wayward Babe,
And she a weeping Woman Old.
Then many a Lover wanders here;
The Sun & Stars are nearer roll'd.

The trees bring forth sweet Extacy
To all who in the desert roam;
Till many a City there is Built,
And many a pleasant Shepherd's home.

But when they find the frowning Babe,
Terror strikes thro' the region wide;
They cry "The Babe! The Babe is Born!"
And flee away on Every side.

For who dare touch the frowning form,
His arm is wither'd to its root;
Lions, Bears, Wolves, all howling flee,
And every Tree does shed its fruit.

And none can touch that frowning form,
Except it be a Woman Old;
She nails him down upon the Rock,
And all is done as I have told.

— *William Blake*

Made in the USA
Middletown, DE
20 November 2020